The Illustrated Rules of
TENNIS

By Wanda Tym
Illustrated by Paul Zuehlke

Ideals Children's Books • Nashville, Tennessee

To Bill, with thanks.
                        —W.T.

To my daughter, Courtney.
                        —P.Z.

Published by Ideals Children's Books
An imprint of Hambleton-Hill Publishing, Inc.
Nashville, Tennessee 37218

Printed and bound in Mexico

Library of Congress Cataloging-in-Publication Data
Tym, Wanda.
    The illustrated rules of tennis / by Wanda Tym ; illustrated by Paul Zuehlke.
        p.   cm.
    ISBN 1-57102-016-0
    1. Tennis—Rules—Juvenile literature. [1. Tennis—Rules.] I. Zuehlke, Paul, ill. II. Title.
GV1001.T95   1995
796.342'02'022—dc20   94-32774
                                                                  CIP
                                                                  AC

Reviewed and endorsed by the National Public Parks Tennis Association (NPPTA).

NPPTA members include tennis clubs, teams, associations, and recreation departments which seek to promote tennis at the public parks level.

Table of Contents

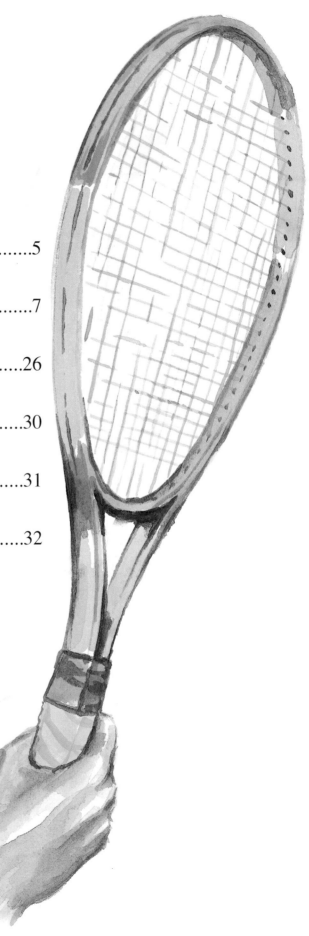

Note to Parents:

This book was designed to introduce young players to the basic rules of tennis and to facilitate discussion of the game by players, coaches, and parents.

The basic rules of the game are presented in a simplified form that can be easily understood by young players. Each rule is accompanied by an accurate, detailed illustration for added clarity. Information was selected for inclusion on the basis of what would be of most interest to young players and their parents.

Written by an experienced tennis coach, the rules in this book were drawn from the author's own tennis experience and from the official rules set forth by the United States Tennis Association (USTA).

The Game of Tennis

Tennis began as a sport played by nobility during the thirteenth century in France. It was played on an indoor court, and the ball was hit not with a racket but with the palm of the hand. Near the end of the sixteenth century, tennis spread to England, probably as a result of marriages between the two countries' royal families. King Edward III of England even built a tennis court inside Windsor Castle.

Tennis first came to the United States in the late 1800s. It began as a sport for the wealthy, who had the time to play and the money to belong to the exclusive clubs.

Today, tennis is popular all over the world. It is played by people of all ages, from young children to senior citizens.

In the modern game of tennis, players stand on either side of a net and use rackets to hit a ball back and forth over the net.

The Rules of the Game

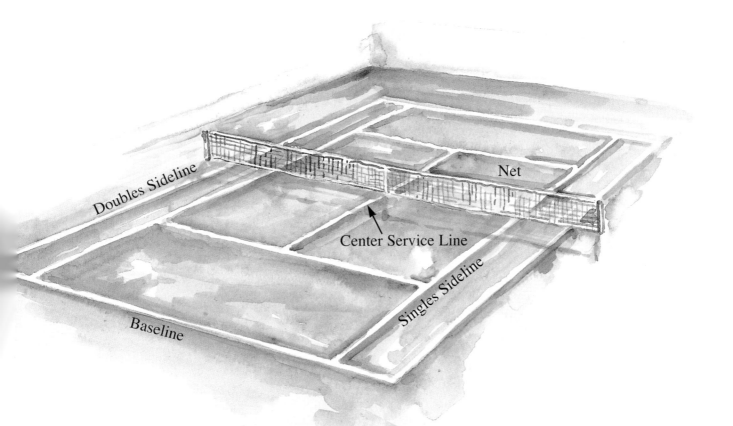

Doubles Sideline

Net

Center Service Line

Singles Sideline

Baseline

Rule 1: The Court

In tennis, the playing field is called a **court**. The tennis court is in the shape of a rectangle, and its size never varies. It is 78 feet long. For a singles match it is 27 feet wide, and for a doubles match it is 36 feet wide (see Rule 7). The surface of the court may be made of cement, asphalt, small gravels, grass, or clay. Because tennis is a year-round sport, courts may be either indoors or outdoors.

Rule 2: The Ball

The standard size tennis ball is 8 inches in **circumference** (the distance around the outside of the ball). It is a hollow, pressurized ball made from rubber and covered with felt. Most balls are bright "optic" yellow in color, which makes them easier to see under most conditions. Some players prefer to use white balls, and white balls are used in some tournaments.

Rule 3: The Net

A **center net** separates the court into two areas. Each area has two **service boxes**, a **baseline**, **singles sidelines**, and **doubles sidelines** (see Rule 17). The net is attached to metal posts at both sides of the court. Heavy nylon rope is usually used to make the net, although some nets are made with metal chains. The net is 3 feet high in the center and $3^1/2$ feet high at the sides where it attaches to the supports. In the center of the net, there is a strap which allows the center height to be adjusted if necessary.

Rule 4: The Racket

Tennis rackets may be made from a variety of materials including fiberglass, ceramic, graphite, boron, or a mixture of any of these materials. Wood may also be used, but it is less common. Rackets usually weigh about 13 to 14 ounces. A standard adult racket is about 27 inches long, while a racket for a junior player may be 2 to 4 inches shorter.

The **head** is the part of the racket which contains the strings. The **grip** is the part of the racket around which the hands are placed. Both the head and the grip may vary in size.

Racket **strings** may be made from either natural or synthetic materials. Natural strings are called **gut**. The strings are woven into the racket through holes in the side. New racket strings are put in as the old ones wear out.

Rule 5: Clothing

The clothing worn by tennis players has changed a lot over the years. In the early 1900s, men wore long pants, long-sleeved shirts, and sometimes straw hats. Women wore hats and long, layered dresses. The clothing was always white.

As tennis became more popular and fashions changed, the clothing worn by tennis players changed as well. Today's tennis players no longer have to wear all-white clothing on the court. They can choose from a wide range of colorful, lightweight sports clothing. The most important thing to remember is to choose clothing that is comfortable and does not restrict movement.

Early 1900s

Rule 6: Shoes

Players usually prefer to wear shoes made especially for playing tennis rather than shoes made for running or aerobics. Tennis shoes provide better support and help prevent ankle and foot injuries. They are also designed to be used on the special surfaces of tennis courts. Some running shoes can leave permanent marks on the courts.

Players usually wear socks with thick, padded bottoms. These socks help to absorb some of the shock of running on the hard surface of the court.

Contemporary
Tennis Clothing

11

Rule 7: The Players

Tennis can be played by two people or by four people. When two people play on a court, it is called a **singles match**, or **singles**. When four people play on a court, it is called a **doubles match**, or **doubles**.

Player substitutions are not allowed during play. The two or four people who begin a match must continue playing until the outcome of the match has been decided.

Rule 8: Server and Receiver

The player serving the ball is called the **server** (see Rule 15).

The player to whom the ball is served is called the **receiver**.

Rule 9: Scoring

The game of tennis is scored in an unusual way. The points are counted a 15, 30, 40, and then game.

The first point won by a player is calle 15. The other player with no points is said to have love, which is the term us in tennis to mean zero points. If the ne point is won by the player who scored first, the score becomes 30–love. If the players have one point each, the score said to be 15–15 or 15–all. The next point, following 30, is 40. The point after that is game, or the point that win the game.

The server usually calls out the score before serving the ball. The server's score is always called first, followed by the receiver's score.

Rule 10: Deuce and Advantage

If each player wins three points so that the game is tied at 40–40, the score is said to be **deuce**. The player who wins the next point is said to have the **advantage**, or **ad**.

If the server has the advantage, it is called **ad in.** If the receiver has the advantage, it is called **ad out**.

If the player who has the advantage wins the next point, he or she wins the game. If not, the score goes back to deuce. In other words, the player who wins two points after deuce is called the winner of the game.

Rule 11: Game, Set, and Match

Tennis is playcd in games, sets, and matches. A **game** is won by the first player to score at least four points and at least two more points than his or her opponent (see Rules 9 and 10).

A **set** is won by the first player to win at least six games and to win at least two more games than his or her opponent.

To win the **match**, the player must win two out of three sets. In some professional tournaments, the player must win three out of five sets.

Rule 12: Winning a Point

A player may win points either by his or her own good play or by the other player's errors. A player will score a point by:

1. Hitting the ball into an area of the court from which the other player cannot return, or hit back, the ball before it bounces twice
2. Serving the ball so accurately that the other player cannot return the ball; this is called an **ace serve** or simply an **ace**

A player's opponent will win a point if a player does one of the following:

1. Returns the ball into the net
2. Returns the ball outside of the lines
3. Gets hit by the ball on any part of his or her body or equipment, except for the racket
4. Touches the net with the racket during a stroke
5. Hits the ball before it passes over the net
6. Hits a ball more than once during a point
7. Catches the ball before it bounces
8. Double faults while serving (see Rule 16)

Rule 13: Starting the Match

Players usually begin by warming up. They do this by hitting balls back and forth to each other for five to ten minutes. When the players are ready to begin the game, they will have a toss. This is similar to tossing a coin, except the racket is used instead of a coin. One player spins the racket on its head on the ground. The other player will make a call, usually saying "up" or "down." This refers to whether the brand-name imprint on the racket handle will land facing up or down.

The player who wins the toss must then make a decision. He or she may choose whether to serve or receive first, in which case the other player will choose the side of the court on which he or she will begin the game. Or the winner of the toss may choose the side of the court on which to begin the game, and the other player will choose whether to serve or receive first. A third option is for the winner of the toss to ask the other player to make the first decision. As soon as the decisions are made, the players take their positions on the court.

Rule 14: Play Is Continuous

There is no time limit in a tennis match. The rule is that play will be continuous until the match is finished. However, there are times when a player can stop to get a drink, to towel off, or to catch his or her breath. The following are the allowed breaks in play.

1. Players have no more than 30 seconds between points and 60 seconds after even games (games 2, 4, 6, and so on).
2. After odd games (games 1, 3, 5, and so on), players have 90 seconds.
3. Between the second and third sets, most players take a 10-minute break. Because no substitutions are allowed, the same two (or four) players must continue playing until the match is completed.
4. Play may be stopped in mid-point if a ball from another court rolls onto the playing court. If this happens, the player must say "let" to stop play, and the point is then replayed.
5. Play may be stopped if someone walks behind the court during play.

19

Rule 15: Service

The **service** begins the play at the start of each game and after each point is scored. For his or her first serve, the server stands behind the baseline as shown in the illustration. The server then hits the first ball over the net and into the service box on his or her left, called the **deuce court**. After the point is finished, the server then moves to the left of the center service line and serves the ball into the service box on his or her right, called the **ad court**. The serves then alternate from the right and left of the center service line until the game is completed.

After each odd game—games 1, 3, 5, and so on—the players switch sides of the court.

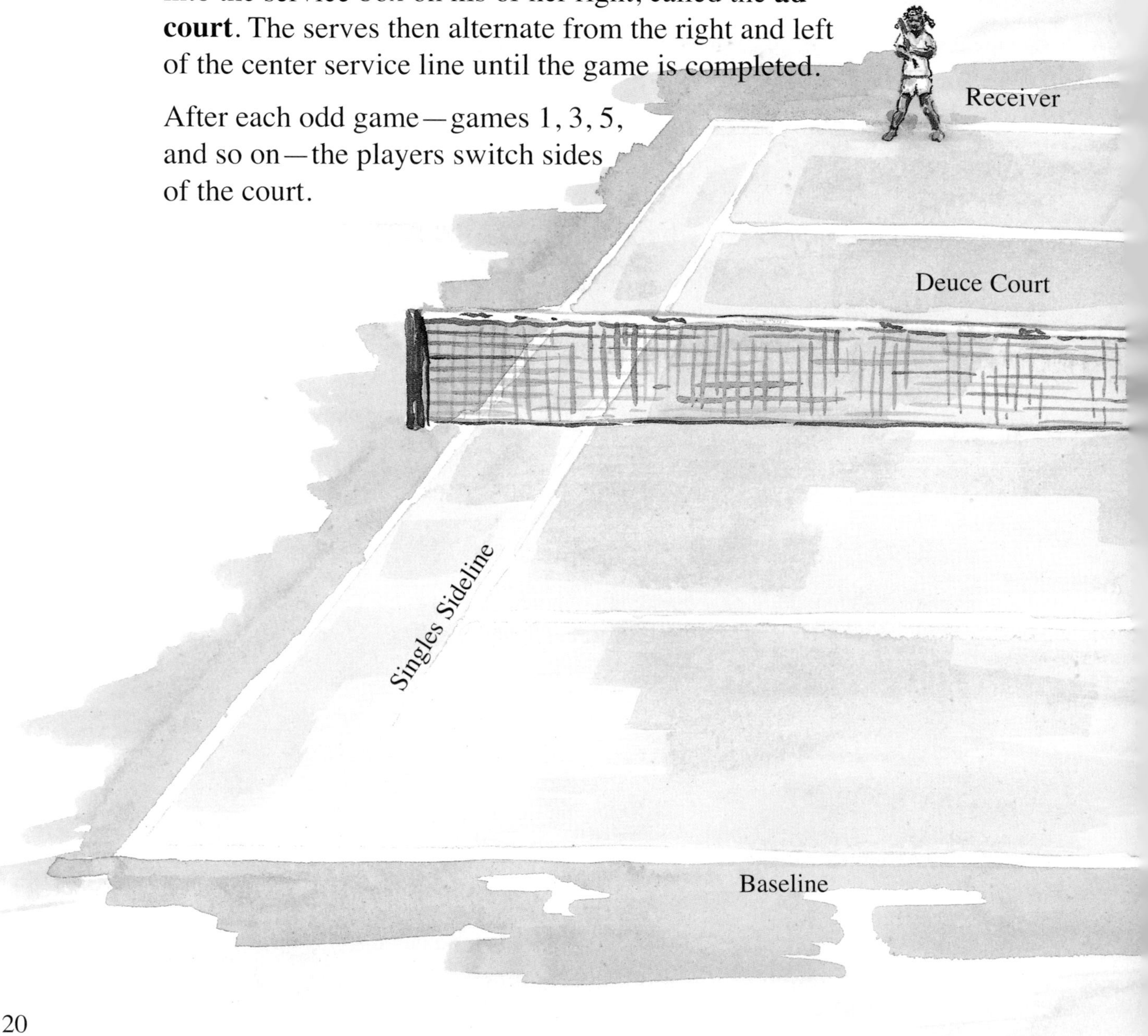

Receiver

Deuce Court

Singles Sideline

Baseline

Rule 16: Service Faults

Servers have two chances to put the ball into the correct service box. If the first serve does not go into the correct box, it is called a **fault**. If the second serve does not go in, it is a **double fault** and a point is awarded to the receiver. A let (see Rule 20) does not count as a fault. If the ball hits the net and goes outside the correct court, it is a fault.

Ad Court

Singles Sideline

Server

Rule 17: The Lines

There are three types of boundary line on the tennis court—the baselines, the service lines, and the sidelines.

The **singles sidelines** are used when two people are playing, and the **doubles sidelines** are used when four people are playing. These lines are the guides which are used to decide if a ball is in or out of play. The doubles sidelines are placed $4\frac{1}{2}$ feet beyond the singles sidelines.

Rule 18: Calling the Lines

Players are on their honor to call balls in or out of play. Except for some tournament matches and professional matches, there are no officials on the court during play. Therefore, it is important to be careful and honest. A player calls balls in or out of play on his or her own side of the court only. These calls are known as **line calls**.

If a ball is hit inside of the lines or if it hits one of the lines, play must continue. If a player is not sure whether the ball is in or out, he or she should continue play.

Ball In

If the player is certain that the ball was out, he or she should make the call immediately by saying "Out" or by making a pointing motion with the forefinger.

If the opponent hits a ball which the player cannot reach, he or she should say "Good" or make a hand motion with the palm down toward the court.

Doubles Sideline

Singles Sideline

Ball Out
(for singles)

Rule 19: Penalties

Penalties are always called by either a match umpire or a tournament official. They are not called by the players. However, there are usually no umpires on the court during a match. If a player feels that penalties might be needed, he or she must leave the court and ask for a tournament official to come and call the match.

A **point penalty** might be called against a player for poor sportsmanship, reporting late for a match, or a foot fault. If a point penalty is called, then the player's opponent is awarded one point.

A **game penalty** may be called for a second instance of poor sportsmanship. If this should happen, the player automatically loses the game.

A **default** occurs for the third instance of poor sportsmanship or for reporting for a match more than fifteen minutes after the scheduled time of the match. A match default means that the player automatically loses the entire match.

Rule 20: Let

If the player is serving and the ball touches the net before dropping into the receiver's service box, it is called a **let**, and the serve is replayed.

Strokes

1. The Serve

The **serve** begins play at the start of each game and after each point is scored (see Rule 15). The server stands behind the baseline, facing the ad court (see pages 20–21). The server must have both feet behind the baseline before hitting the ball; otherwise, a foot fault may be called. The server first checks to see that the receiver is ready. Then the server tosses the ball up into the air and hits it with the racket before the ball touches the ground. The ball must go across the net and land in the service area diagonally opposite from the server's position. If a ball does not land in the correct service area, it is a fault (see Rule 16).

Volley

Overhead

2. Overhead and Volley

Overheads and volleys are hit in the air before the ball bounces. A **volley** is any shot made by hitting the ball before it bounces, while an **overhead** is a hard hit made from above the head.

As with ground strokes, players may hit either forehand or backhand. Volleys and overheads are usually hit when the player is closer to the net. Players usually hit more volleys in doubles play than in singles.

3. Ground Strokes

A **ground stroke** is used to hit the ball after it has bounced on the court.

A **forehand ground stroke** is hit with the palm of the hand which is gripping the racket facing toward the net. For a right-handed player, it is played on the right side of the body. For a left-handed player, it is played on the left side of the body.

A **backhand ground stroke** may be hit with either one hand or two hands gripping the racket. It is hit so that the back of the front hand faces the net. For a right-handed player, it is played on the left side of the body. For a left-handed player, it is played on the right side.

Players may choose to hit either a forehand or backhand on any ground stroke. Ground strokes are usually used when players are in the backcourt, but may also be used when a ball bounces inside the service box.

Backhand Ground Stroke

Forehand Ground Stroke

Sportsmanship in the Game of Tennis

Tennis is a game of etiquette, or good manners, and good sportsmanship. Players should always try to be polite and considerate of other players—but sometimes disagreements may occur, especially when players are calling the lines.

Because players often call their own matches without the help of officials, they are on their honor to make the correct call. If a player does not agree with a line call made by an opponent, the player should ask if he or she is certain of the call. If the opponent's answer is yes, play must continue. If this situation occurs during a tournament, the player may wish to go to the desk and ask for an official to come to the court.

If players disagree on the score, they should go back to the last score on which they both agree or spin a racket.

Here are some other simple guidelines for showing good sportsmanship. During warmup, players should not attempt to hit balls away from each other. A player should never throw a racket or slam a ball into the net or fence. Abusive language and yelling are not good behavior. Stalling between points or between games does not show a good playing attitude. After the last point, players should come to the net quickly and shake hands. A player should always be polite and congratulate his or her opponent, no matter who won.

Summary of the Rules of Tennis

Rule 1: The Court
The tennis court is in the shape of a rectangle. It is 78 feet long and 27 feet wide for a singles match or 36 feet wide for a doubles match.

Rule 2: The Ball
The standard size tennis ball is 8 inches in circumference. It is a hollow, pressurized ball made from rubber and covered with felt. Most balls are bright "optic" yellow in color.

Rule 3: The Net
A center net separates the court into two areas. Each area has two service boxes, a baseline, singles sidelines, and doubles sidelines. The net is 3 feet high in the center and $3\frac{1}{2}$ feet high at the sides.

Rule 4: The Racket
Tennis rackets usually weigh about 13 to 14 ounces. A standard adult racket is about 27 inches long, while a racket for a junior player may be 2 to 4 inches shorter.

Rule 5: Clothing
Tennis players no longer have to wear all-white clothing on the court. It is important to choose clothing that is comfortable and does not restrict movement.

Rule 6: Shoes
Players usually prefer to wear shoes made especially for playing tennis because they provide better support and help prevent ankle and foot injuries.

Rule 7: The Players
Tennis can be played by two people, called singles, or by four people, called doubles.

Rule 8: Server and Receiver
The player serving the ball is called the server. The player to whom the ball is served is called the receiver.

Rule 9: Scoring
In tennis, the points are counted as 15, 30, 40, and then game. Love is the term used to mean zero points.

Rule 10: Deuce and Advantage
If the game is tied at 40–40, the score is said to be deuce. The player who wins the next point is said to have the advantage, or ad.

Rule 11: Game, Set, and Match
A game is won by the first player to score at least four points and at least two points more than the opponent. A set is won by the first player to win at least six games and at least two games more than the opponent. The first player to win two sets wins the match.

Rule 12: Winning a Point
A player will score a point if the opponent is unable to properly return the ball over the net.

Rule 13: Starting the Match
When the players are ready to begin the game, one player will spin the racket to decide who will serve first and from which side of the court each player will begin the game.

Rule 14: Play Is Continuous
There is no time limit in a tennis match. Except for brief breaks, play must be continuous until the match is finished.

Rule 15: Service
The service begins the play at the start of each game and after each point is scored.

Rule 16: Service Faults
Servers have two chances to put the ball into the correct service box. If the first serve does not go into the correct box, it is a fault. If the second serve does not go in, it is a double fault, and a point is awarded to the receiver.

Rule 17: The Lines
There are three types of boundary line on the tennis court—the baselines, the service lines, and the sidelines.

Rule 18: Calling the Lines
Players are on their honor to call balls in or out of play. Players make line calls on their own side of the court only.

Rule 19: Penalties
Penalties are always called by either a match umpire or a tournament official. Penalties may be called for poor sportsmanship, reporting late for a match, or a foot fault.

Rule 20: Let
If the player is serving and the ball touches the net before dropping into the receiver's service box, it is called a let, and the serve is replayed.

Vocabulary of the Game

ace: a serve hit so accurately that the other player cannot return it

advantage: also called **ad**; the point after deuce or 40–40; if the server has the advantage, it's called **ad in**; if the receiver has the advantage, it's called **ad out**

backhand: a ground stroke hit with the back of the hand going toward the net

deuce: a score of 40–40, when each player has won at least 3 points; the score of deuce can occur several times in the same game

double fault: a player is unable to serve the ball into the correct service box on two attempts; the receiver is awarded a point

doubles: a game with four players on the court, two on each team

fault: a serve which does not land in the correct service box

foot fault: a penalty called if the server steps on the baseline or into the court when serving the ball

forehand: a ground stroke hit with the palm of the hand going toward the net

let: the term used when a ball has been served into the correct service box but has hit the top of the net; also used when there has been interference with play

out: a ball landing outside the lines

love: zero points

overhead: a stroke hit with the racket above the head; usually hit before the ball bounces

rally: when players hit the ball back and forth successfully, usually during warmup or practice

volley: a stroke hit by the player before the ball touches the ground